Money matters

Understanding the psychological landscape of wealth

By

Bill P. Beck

TABLE OF CONTENTS

INTRODUCTION

Welcome to the captivating world of "Money Matters: Understanding the Psychological Landscape of Wealth." In this illuminating exploration, we venture beyond traditional finance guides, delving into the intricate tapestry of the human mind and its profound influence on our relationship with wealth.

This book is not your typical financial manual; it's a deep dive into the subconscious forces that shape our financial decisions.

From the early imprints of money experiences to the intricate dance between emotions and financial choices, we navigate the labyrinth of our psychological landscape to uncover the hidden drivers of our financial destiny.

Through engaging narratives, real-world examples, and expert insights, "Money Matters" transforms the way we perceive and manage money. It challenges preconceived notions and invites readers to embark on a transformative journey toward a healthier money mindset.

Join us as we unravel the mysteries of the mind's role in matters of wealth, offering not just practical strategies but a profound understanding of the forces shaping our financial lives.

"Money Matters" is more than a book; it's an invitation to rethink, redefine, and reimagine your relationship with money for a richer and more fulfilling future.

CHAPTER ONE

Unveiling the Connection Between Psychology and Finances

The complicated dance between psychology and finances is a fascinating dynamic that greatly impacts our decision-making processes, economic habits, and overall financial well-being. As we dive into the depths of this link, we unravel the psychological aspects that influence our financial decisions and affect the outcomes of our financial undertakings.

1. Behavioral Economics: Understanding Irrationality in Financial Decision-Making

The area of behavioral economics has exposed the illogical features of human decision-making when it comes to finances.

Cognitive biases, such as loss aversion, anchoring, and overconfidence, can drive individuals to make poor choices, harming their financial stability. Recognizing and managing these biases is key to making effective financial decisions.

2. Emotional Influences on Investment Behavior

Emotions have a significant influence on financial decision-making, particularly in the field of investing. Fear and greed may drive market patterns, leading to bubbles or collapses. Investors' emotional responses to market volatility frequently result in impulsive decisions, harming long-term financial goals.

Developing emotional intelligence is crucial to handling the turbulent nature of financial markets.

3. Financial stress's effect on mental health

Stress related to money can have a negative impact on mental health. Anxiety and despair might be exacerbated by persistent worries about finances, debt, or employment security. Understanding the psychological toll of financial stress underlines the significance of financial knowledge and preparation to develop resilience and mental well-being.

4. Money Scripts: Uncovering Subconscious Beliefs about Money

Money scripts are established views about money developed in infancy that impact financial attitudes and habits. Exploring and questioning these scripts can lead to a healthy relationship with money. Recognizing the influence of upbringing on financial views helps individuals modify their financial narratives and make better-informed decisions.

5. The Power of Financial Education in Shaping Behavior

Financial education is a vital tool in ending the cycle of poor financial decisions.

Empowering individuals with information about budgeting, investing and debt management boosts their financial literacy. Education also plays a role in establishing a mindset of long-term financial planning rather than succumbing to short-term desires.

6. Cultural and societal influences on financial behavior

Cultural and community standards substantially impact financial behaviors. Understanding how cultural expectations impact spending habits, saving patterns, and investment decisions gives insights into why individuals may depart from sensible economic choices.

Cultural knowledge is vital in providing financial advice and solutions to varied communities.

7. The Psychology of Consumerism and Advertising

Consumerism is strongly ingrained in psychology, pushed by advertising and cultural forces. Examining the psychological strategies deployed by marketers sheds light on how aspirations for status, acceptability, and enjoyment influence customer behavior. Recognizing these effects encourages individuals to make more conscious and attentive purchasing choices.

CHAPTER TWO

The Roots of Money Mindset

Our connection with money is profoundly rooted and formed by a complicated network of experiences, influences, and cultural variables. The phrase "money mindset" includes the ideas, attitudes, and emotions individuals have about money, impacting their financial decisions and behaviors. To properly comprehend and modify one's money mindset, it's vital to study the sources of these deeply established attitudes.

1. Cultural and Socioeconomic Context: Shaping Financial Perspectives

The cultural and social context in which we grow up has a key influence on establishing our financial perspective.

Cultural norms around spending, saving, and investing, as well as society's expectations around wealth and success, impact the values we attach to money. Understanding the influence of these external variables helps individuals detect and fight any limiting ideas that may inhibit financial progress.

1. Educational Influences: The Role of Formal and Informal Learning

Formal schooling and informal learning contribute considerably to the formation of our financial thinking. Financial education or the lack thereof, influences our knowledge of budgeting, investing, and financial planning.

Additionally, informal learning through experiences, talks, and exposure to diverse financial circumstances shapes our attitudes towards risk, success, and failure.

2. Media and Advertising: Shaping Consumer Behavior

Media, advertising, and popular culture exert a strong impact on our money attitudes. The frequent exposure to messages encouraging consumerism, materialism, and cultural expectations of money might alter our judgments of financial success. Analyzing the effect of media narratives helps individuals discriminate between external pressures and their underlying financial values.

3. Traumatic Financial Experiences: Impact on Money Mindset

Traumatic financial situations, such as bankruptcy, job loss, or economic challenges, may leave a permanent mark on our financial thinking. These events may lead to dread, scarcity thinking, or a heightened aversion to financial risk. Recognizing and processing the emotional implications of these situations is vital for altering one's relationship with money and creating resilience.

4. Peer and Social Influences: The Power of Social Circles

The people we surround ourselves with, including friends, coworkers, and social circles, affect our financial perspective.

Peer pressure, societal comparisons, and shared financial values can either strengthen or challenge our previous ideas. Building an understanding of these social effects helps individuals make financial decisions consistent with their personal ideals rather than submitting to external pressures.

Exploring Childhood Influences on Financial Behavior

Childhood experiences serve as the foundation for many facets of our adult lives, including our relationship with money. The dynamics within our families, the financial practices we see, and the teachings provided during formative years contribute considerably to the formation of our financial behavior. This research dives into the enormous impact of formative influences on our financial attitudes, decision-making processes, and general financial well-being.

1. Family Dynamics and Financial Modeling: The Power of Observation

Children are good observers, gathering information from their immediate environment.

The way parents handle money, talk about finances, and make financial decisions acts as a blueprint for children's future habits. Positive financial modeling may inculcate healthy financial habits, whereas negative patterns may continue a cycle of bad financial decision-making.

2. Financial Education at Home: The Role of Parental Guidance

Parents operate as the primary educators in a child's upbringing, and this extends to financial education. Conversations about budgeting, saving, and appropriate spending provide youngsters with fundamental knowledge. Lack of financial literacy or poor financial behaviors at home may contribute to a restricted grasp of money management.

3. Money Scripts: Internalizing Beliefs from Childhood

Psychologists refer to "money scripts" as the internalized ideas and attitudes about money established throughout childhood. These scripts, sometimes unconscious, impact financial views and behaviors. Whether it's a belief in plenty, scarcity, or the moral consequences of riches, knowing and confronting these scripts is vital for establishing a good money attitude.

4. Financial Stress and Childhood Anxiety: Long-term Impacts

Childhood experiences of financial hardship or volatility can have lifelong consequences for a person's connection with money.

The worry and uncertainty associated with economic adversity may lead to habits such as overspending or an aversion to risk throughout maturity.

Addressing and recovering from these early traumas is vital for creating a better financial foundation.

5. Pocket Money and Early Financial Responsibility: Lessons in Budgeting

The distribution of pocket money or allowances gives parents an opportunity to teach youngsters about budgeting and responsible spending. Learning to handle a restricted quantity of money improves financial responsibility and decision-making abilities. These early lessons led to the formation of a sense of financial discipline.

6. Educational Initiatives: Integrating Financial Literacy in Schools

Formal education, including school curriculum and extracurricular programs, has a crucial influence on influencing financial practices.

Financial literacy programs in schools equip students with real-world knowledge and abilities for budgeting, decision-making, and future financial planning. Educational programs bridge the gap for people whose families may not provide complete financial assistance.

7. Cultural and Socioeconomic Context: Influences Beyond the Family

Beyond the family, cultural and social variables may shape a child's financial outlook. Societal expectations, cultural views towards money and economic inequality contribute to the varied variety of financial perspectives youngsters face. Recognizing and appreciating these wider impacts offers perspective on the range of financial actions witnessed in maturity.

CHAPTER THREE

Investing with the Mind in Mind

Understanding how emotions, biases, and cognitive processes affect financial decisions is vital for attaining long-term success in the market. Here are some crucial themes and insights for investors to consider:

1. Emotional Intelligence:

Successful investors acquire emotional intelligence to control their emotions efficiently. Fear and greed can lead to rash judgments and market timing blunders. Being mindful of one's emotional condition and keeping discipline are keys to making smart financial decisions.

2. Behavioral Finance:

Behavioral finance investigates how psychological elements impact financial behaviors. Concepts like loss aversion, overconfidence, and herd mentality can dramatically affect investing choices. Recognizing these biases helps investors make more rational judgments.

3. Long-Term Perspective:

Investing with the mind in mind entails having a long-term view. Short-term market changes can be emotionally distressing, but a focus on the intrinsic worth of investments over time can help ride out volatility.

4. Risk Management:

Understanding one's risk tolerance and maintaining a diverse portfolio are key components of investing properly.

Risk management entails balancing prospective profits with the degree of risk one is comfortable incurring.

5. Mindful Investing:

Mindfulness approaches, such as meditation and self-reflection, can help decision-making by developing a calm and concentrated mentality. Practicing mindfulness helps investors stay present and make reasonable choices rather than respond emotionally to market volatility.

6. Continuous Learning:

Successful investors are lifelong learners. Keeping current with market trends, economic statistics, and industry advancements helps investors make educated judgments.

This continuing education also involves understanding the psychological components of investing.

7. Contrarian Thinking:

Going against the crowd may be a great approach. When the bulk of investors are influenced by emotions or market trends, contrarian investors may identify opportunities in undervalued assets. This strategy involves discipline and a firm belief in one's analysis.

8. Adaptability:

Markets are dynamic and susceptible to change. Successful investors modify their strategy based on altering economic conditions, market movements, and geopolitical issues.

Flexibility and the capacity to respond to new knowledge are crucial traits.

9. Financial Planning:

Developing a thorough financial plan that corresponds with personal goals and risk tolerance is a core part of investing with the mind in mind. This strategy provides a roadmap for financial decisions and helps investors stay focused on their long-term objectives.

10. Professional Guidance:

Seeking counsel from financial specialists can provide significant insights and direction. Financial advisers may offer an objective viewpoint, helping investors handle emotional problems and make well-informed decisions.

Understanding Cognitive Biases in Financial Investments

Investing in financial markets is a difficult effort that involves not only a profound study of economic concepts but also an awareness of the psychological elements that might impact decision-making. Cognitive biases, or persistent patterns of deviation from norm or rationality in judgment, sometimes play a substantial influence in molding investing decisions. In this investigation, we dig into the subtleties of cognitive biases in the area of financial investing and explain how investors might manage these psychological hazards to make more informed and sensible choices.

1. Overcoming Overconfidence:

One prevalent cognitive bias in financial investments is overconfidence. Investors often overestimate their talents, prompting them to take on unnecessary risks or miss vital information. Recognizing and overcoming overconfidence includes adopting a more humble and realistic view of one's own talents. Regularly reassessing one's investment plan and obtaining external feedback might help lessen the influence of this bias.

2. Loss Aversion and the Fear of Missing Out (FOMO)

Loss aversion, the tendency to prioritize avoiding losses above earning equal gains, and the fear of missing out (FOMO) might cause investors to make inefficient decisions. Understanding that losses are a normal aspect of investing and establishing a disciplined approach to decision-making can help limit these biases. Diversification and a long-term investing perspective are crucial techniques to offset the influence of these biases.

3. Anchoring and Adjustment:

Anchoring happens when investors focus on certain reference points, such as previous prices or expert projections, and make decisions based on these anchors. This prejudice can lead to bad investment choices. Counteracting anchoring entails completing comprehensive research, evaluating many views, and minimizing dependence on single data points.

Regularly reassessing and revising investing decisions might help break free from entrenched positions.

4. Confirmation Bias:

Confirmation bias includes giving priority to information that supports pre-existing opinions while ignoring conflicting evidence. This bias might hamper objective decision-making in financial ventures. Investors should actively seek out alternative opinions, question their preconceptions, and have a critical mentality while reviewing information. A well-rounded approach to research and analysis can help limit the influence of confirmation bias.

5. Regret Aversion:

Regret aversion can emerge as a hesitation to make decisions owing to a fear of making the wrong option.

This can lead to lost opportunities and inefficient portfolio management. Investors should realize that not all judgments will be ideal and focus on making educated choices based on comprehensive study and analysis. Embracing a learning mentality can help overcome the dread of regret.

CHAPTER FOUR

Emotions and Financial Decision-Making

Emotions have a deep influence on defining our everyday lives, influencing our relationships, and even affecting our financial decisions. In the domain of finance, where rationality and logic are typically regarded as crucial, emotions may be both a driving force and a dangerous disaster. This article digs into the complicated interplay between emotions and financial decision-making, analyzing how psychological elements may impact investing choices and influence overall financial well-being.

1. The Psychological Landscape of Financial Decision-Making:

Understanding the psychological basis of financial decisions is vital for investors. Behavioral economics illustrates how cognitive biases, heuristics, and emotions may drive individuals to depart from strictly rational decision-making. Key psychological aspects include loss aversion, overconfidence, and the fear of missing out (FOMO), all of which can greatly affect investing choices.

2. Fear and Greed: The Emotional Roller Coaster of Market Volatility

Financial markets are naturally volatile, vulnerable to unforeseen movements that elicit intense emotions among investors.

The dread of losses and the attraction of prospective gains can stimulate hasty decision-making, leading to purchasing high and selling low. Understanding the psychology underlying market changes can equip investors to handle volatility with a more reasonable approach.

3. Emotional Intelligence in Financial Management:

Emotional intelligence (EI) is the capacity to identify, analyze, and control one's own emotions as well as those of others. In the context of financial decision-making, people with high emotional intelligence are better suited to make reasoned decisions, resist impulsive behaviors, and handle market risks.

Developing emotional intelligence becomes a crucial advantage for investors seeking long-term financial success.

4. The Role of Stress on Financial Decision-Making:

Stress is a formidable force that may obscure judgment and impair decision-making abilities. The financial environment regularly exposes individuals to high-stress events, such as market downturns or economic crises. Recognizing the influence of stress on decision-making and implementing stress management practices can help investors make better-informed and resilient choices.

5. Robo-Advisors and Emotion-Free Investing:

The development of robo-advisors presents a technical solution aimed at reducing the role of emotions in financial decision-making. These automated investment systems leverage algorithms and data-driven methodologies to make objective, emotion-free selections. While robo-advisors provide advantages in terms of impartiality, they also raise issues about the importance of human intuition and emotional intelligence in the investment process.

Managing Fear, Greed, and Emotional Triggers

Managing fear, greed, and emotional triggers is vital for making informed decisions, especially in areas like money, investment, and general personal well-being. Here's some high-quality material about how to handle these emotions:

Understanding Fear, Greed, and Emotional Triggers

1. Recognizing emotional triggers:

Awareness is the first step. Understand the conditions or factors that elicit fear or greed. It may be market volatility, financial instability, or the fear of missing out (FOMO).

2. The Psychology Behind Fear and Greed:

Dive into the psychological implications of fear and greed. Fear frequently arises from the unknown or prospective losses, whereas greed might arise from the desire for immediate profits. Knowing these triggers might help you stay sensible.

3. Importance of Emotional Intelligence:

Develop emotional intelligence to better regulate your responses. This entails identifying your emotions, comprehending their significance, and learning to respond rather than react impulsively.

Strategies for Managing Fear

1. Educate Yourself:

Knowledge is a strong tool against fear. The more you learn about the market, investments, or any circumstance producing worry, the more confident and in control you'll feel.

2. Establish a Rational Perspective:

Challenge illogical thoughts. Ask yourself if your anxieties are founded on facts or assumptions. Often, anxieties might be overblown, and a reasonable viewpoint can help calm your emotions.

3. Have a plan:

Create a well-thought-out plan for many eventualities.

Knowing what to do in preparation might lessen anxiety when presented with unexpected scenarios.

Strategies for Managing Greed

1. Set realistic goals.

Define reasonable and achievable financial objectives. Greed typically occurs when individuals pursue unrealistic profits. Having defined objectives might help you stay focused and grounded.

2. Diversify Your Portfolio:

Diversification is a crucial technique to reduce risks linked to greed. Spread your investments among several assets to avoid placing all your eggs in one basket.

3. Stick to a disciplined approach:

Implement a systematic investment approach and prevent impulsive judgments. Greed may entice you to depart from your approach, but discipline is vital for long-term success.

General Strategies for Emotional Management

1. Practice Mindfulness:

Mindfulness approaches, such as meditation, can help you stay present and lessen the influence of emotions on your decision-making process.

2. Surround yourself with a support system:

Discuss your concerns and anxieties with a trustworthy friend, mentor, or financial advisor. Sometimes, an outsider perspective can bring significant insights.

3. Learn from experience:

Reflect on prior events when emotions may have impacted your decisions. Use these lessons to build your emotional resilience for future circumstances.

CHAPTER FIVE

Cultivating a Healthy Money Mindset

A healthy money attitude is vital for financial well-being and success. It goes beyond the numbers in your bank account and extends to your ideas, attitudes, and actions relating to money. Cultivating a good and empowered money mentality may substantially improve your financial path. Here are the fundamental elements to help you establish and maintain a healthy money perspective.

1. Transition from Scarcity to Abundance:

Thinking in terms of scarcity emphasizes limitations, worry, and lack.

Change your mind set to one of abundance by valuing the opportunities and possibilities that surround you.

Practice thankfulness for what you have, acknowledging the wealth in your life beyond only monetary factors.

2. Embrace a Growth Mindset:

Adopt a development mentality in your financial activities. See setbacks as chances to learn and grow rather than insurmountable hurdles.

Understand that your financial status may improve through knowledge, work, and tenacity.

3. Define Your Financial Goals:

Clearly establish your short-term and long-term financial goals. Having a clear vision can help you stay focused and motivated.

Break down huge goals into smaller, doable milestones to make progress more manageable.

4. Budgeting and Financial Planning:

Create a reasonable budget that corresponds with your goals. Track your spending and make educated decisions about where your money goes.

Develop a financial strategy that incorporates saving, investing, and debt management. Having a roadmap offers a sense of control and direction.

5. Mindful Spending Habits:

Practice mindful spending by being deliberate with your purchases. Differentiate between necessities and wants, and make decisions that accord with your beliefs.

Avoid impulsive buying and take time to examine the long-term implications of your financial actions.

6. Value Yourself Beyond Your Net Worth:

Recognize that your self-worth is not determined by your financial balance. Separate your personality from your financial condition.

Focus on establishing a well-rounded and meaningful life, spanning relationships, personal growth, and experiences.

7. Educate yourself about finances:

Knowledge is power. Take the time to educate yourself on personal finance, investing, and financial planning.

Stay educated about economic developments and be proactive in making smart financial decisions.

8. Celebrate financial wins:

Acknowledge and appreciate your financial successes, regardless of their size. This positive reinforcement will help reinforce your good-money perspective.

Share your triumphs with others and build a healthy financial culture.

9. Seek professional guidance.

Consider speaking with financial professionals or consultants for specialized counsel. They can give insights, tactics, and assistance targeted to your individual circumstances.

Don't hesitate to ask questions and actively engage in managing your finances.

10. Practice patience and persistence.

Building riches takes time. Be patient and persistent in your endeavors, especially during hard circumstances.

Learn from setbacks and regard them as chances for progress rather than failures.

Practical Strategies for Financial Wellness

Certainly! Making wise financial decisions and implementing sound money management techniques are necessary to achieve financial wellness. Here are a few doable methods to improve your financial health:

1. Create a budget:

Develop a realistic budget that covers your income, spending, and savings objectives.

Categorize your spending into fixed (rent, utilities) and variable (entertainment, dining out) categories to see where your money is going.

2. Emergency Fund:

Establish an emergency fund to cover unanticipated expenditures like medical crises or auto repairs.

Aim to save three to six months' worth of living costs in a separate, easily accessible account.

3. Debt Management:

Prioritize paying off high-interest debts, such as credit cards, to alleviate financial stress.

Consider debt consolidation to simplify payments and perhaps cut interest rates.

4. Investing for the Future:

Start investing early to take advantage of compound growth.

Diversify your investments to manage risk; explore a combination of stocks, bonds, and other assets based on your risk tolerance and financial goals.

5. Retirement Planning:

Contribute consistently to retirement accounts like 401(k)s or IRAs to ensure your financial future.

Take advantage of employer-sponsored retirement plans, especially if your company makes a matching contribution.

6. Insurance Coverage:

Review and update your insurance coverage frequently, including health, life, and property insurance.

Ensure you have appropriate coverage to defend against unforeseen occurrences that might harm your money.

7. Educate Yourself:

Stay educated about financial topics by reading books, articles, and attending seminars.

Understand the essentials of personal finance, investing, and taxation to make educated decisions.

8. Negotiate and cut expenses:

Regularly analyze your bills and negotiate for better pricing on things like cable, internet, and insurance.

Identify and reduce needless spending to free up money for savings and investing.

9. Continuous Learning:

Stay current on financial trends, economic indicators, and market circumstances to make educated judgments.

Attend classes, webinars, or speak with financial consultants to boost your financial literacy.

10. Set financial goals:

Establish short-term and long-term financial goals to guide your decision-making.

Regularly examine your goals and change your financial strategy as needed.

11. Mindful Spending:

Practice mindful spending by discriminating between needs and wants.

Avoid impulsive purchases and evaluate the long-term consequences of your spending habits.

12. Tax Planning:

Be proactive in your tax preparation to reduce your tax obligation.

Leverage tax-advantaged accounts and take advantage of applicable deductions and credits.

CONCLUSION

In conclusion, "Money Matters: Understanding the Psychological Landscape of Wealth" presents a thorough examination of the delicate link between individuals and their financial well-being. Through thorough study and engaging storytelling, the book digs into the numerous psychological components that govern our views, actions, and decision-making surrounding money. It effectively navigates through the complicated interplay of emotions, societal expectations, and personal beliefs that affect our financial viewpoints.

The author's sophisticated approach goes beyond traditional financial guidance, presenting a complete view of how money affects our self-esteem, relationships, and general fulfillment in life.

By shedding light on the underlying motives behind financial choices, the book helps readers establish a more aware and deliberate relationship with money.

Furthermore, "Money Matters" serves as a great resource for both individuals seeking financial knowledge and specialists in the domains of psychology and finance. The multidisciplinary structure of the book bridges the gap between the practical elements of managing money and the underlying psychological roots, giving it a thorough guide for anybody navigating the complicated landscape of personal finance.

In a world where financial well-being is increasingly acknowledged as a vital component of total pleasure, this book stands out as a source of insight and assistance.

It invites readers to think about their own financial tales, creating deeper knowledge that goes beyond the figures on a balance sheet. Ultimately, "Money Matters" challenges us to begin on a transforming path toward a more thoughtful and meaningful relationship with money, knowing that genuine success extends well beyond the simple amassing of monetary possessions